MARKETING
TO HUMANS

MARKETING TO HUMANS

A CUSTOMER-OBSESSED STRATEGY TO DRIVE CONNECTION AND SALES

IDAN SHPIZEAR

Marketing to Humans: A Customer-Obsessed Strategy to Drive Connection and Sales

ISBN: 9780578876023

First Edition

Cover image: © Vadym Malyshevskyi - 123rf.com
Cover and interior design: Adina Cucicov

CONTENTS

Introduction vii

1. Defining Your Competitive Edge 1

2. Understand the World of Your Client 13

3. Discovering Your Client's Needs 29

4. Breaking Down the Decision-Making Process 43

5. Where Your Passion and Clients Meet 57

6. Where to Find Your Future Clients 67

7. Putting It All Together in a Strategy 81

8. Executing and Optimizing Your Marketing Strategy ... 87

9. Beyond Conversion 99

Next Steps 107

INTRODUCTION

I once hauled a massive sign advertising my business up a steep hillside to snag the attention of drivers on one of L.A.'s busiest freeways. While I still believe in taking bold risks, I'll admit this was not my best idea. For one thing, I wasn't *technically* allowed to post a sign there. For another, I didn't have the tools to do it right. After all the sweat I put into it, the sign toppled over and slid down the hill. The effort may not have been worth the hour of publicity I got out of it.

This early marketing effort is a perfect metaphor for what so many business owners go through as they try to build a reputation and attract clients. They are desperate for more visibility. So they find ways to shout the name of their business more loudly, make the print bigger and the logo splashier. But they don't create a solid foundation that gives meaning to their message. They don't use marketing as an opportunity to connect with clients on a human level.

In the end, they don't accomplish much.

The biggest mistake I see business owners make is that they think "branding" just means slapping their logo on everything. I've made this same error.

When I began my company, I had one carpet cleaning machine. My professional network was miniscule, as I had only been in the U.S. for one year and had virtually no personal history in the region I served. I didn't even have a space of my own. I shared a two bedroom apartment with five other guys, and I used my Volvo as an office.

In other words, slow, organic growth was not going to work for me. I couldn't afford to spend years building a reputation naturally, depending on referrals from the few customers I had. I needed to get the word out, and that meant a huge marketing push.

I sent every building management company in the area a fax introducing myself and my business, promising that if they called today, I'd be there tomorrow to clean their carpets. I covered the San Fernando Valley with I-don't-know-how-many signs reading "Got mold? Call us." When I didn't have a job booked, I parked the company truck on a main street, sometimes paying gas station owners $100 to park outside their business for five hours.

Honestly, these efforts did help me schedule more jobs and grow my business. But the real, exponential growth came when I started advertising on Google.

It was 2003, a time when most business owners considered online marketing a waste of money. Colleagues encouraged me to focus on the Yellow Pages, claiming that the Internet was never going to take off in any meaningful way. But when I overheard a couple guys in a restaurant talking about Google AdWords—a new advertising channel that helped you secure more business faster—I couldn't help myself. It had been a year since I started my carpet cleaning company, and now that I was transitioning into full-service restoration, I needed a bold strategy to match my bold, new mission.

I went home and spent six hours learning everything I could about AdWords. I created my first Google ad that night, and lo and behold, I booked a job *the next morning*. After that, I was booking jobs every single day. I brought on new team members, built new client relationships, and expanded my vision for the company.

Most importantly, I reinvented my approach to marketing.

You see, Google ads did more than help me to reach more people more easily. It also made it easier to test my messaging and learn about my clients. Each time I changed the wording of an ad, I would know in a matter of days how well property owners responded to the new approach.

To put it simply, I got to know my target customer much better… and much faster.

In using a new technology that offered deeper insight into consumer behavior, I came to a game-changing realization:

> → Customers aren't looking for a higher quality of service; they're looking for a higher quality of *life*.

You can brag all day about having the best wet vac on the market, but it's all white noise to your prospective clients. What they really want to know is if you can restore their refuge or ease their stress or quiet their fears.

Once I understood that, everything changed. 911 Restoration grew faster than ever. In less than six years, I was in a position to franchise the business. I was also able to expand my marketing efforts exponentially, ultimately co-founding a separate marketing company with my incredible COO, Miri Offir. We created seamless systems for spreading the word about 911 Restoration from coast to coast, pulling in more business for our franchisees, growing our company name, and expanding our reach. Today, our marketing system generates close to 100,000 leads a year.

My company is where it is today because we learned early on that if you want to reach more clients more effectively, you have to center your strategy around connection and engagement. You have to know your customer, and you have to know *yourself*.

You have to know what your business offers that no other company can. And here's the beauty of it all: *it's not about being the best in your field*. It's about tapping into your unique strengths, passions, and values. It's about connecting your deeper purpose with the emotional needs of your customer. That human connection is priceless.

Think about it. If what you sell is x number of guys putting in x number of hours using equipment you bought for x amount of money, then it's easy for the customer to put a finite dollar amount to the value of your service.

But if what you sell is peace of mind and a better life, you can name your price.

I know marketing is an uncomfortable topic for a lot of business owners in our field. Many of us began as tradespeople, and tradespeople tend to value things like practical skills, professional transparency, and friendly customer service. We think of advertising as a performance or a game of manipulation. We think we have to be eye-catching or artistic or charming. But I am here to tell you that marketing is actually about using the skill set you already have to earn the trust of property owners *honestly*.

They don't care how sleek your website is or how catchy your radio commercials are. They want one thing:

A contractor they can count on to understand and meet their needs.

Your objective in designing a marketing campaign is to show them why you're their best option… to demonstrate that you understand them, you value them, and you can offer something that will make their lives better.

My goal in this book is to show you how you can tap into your strengths to create a strategy that connects you with customers, builds your reputation in the community, and sets you up for exponential, long-term growth. I will teach you how to make small, simple adjustments that generate major leads.

Most importantly, I am going to show you that you already have the skills you need to excel at marketing. What you lack is the perspective to put those skills to work in the most effective way.

And it all begins with knowing your strengths.

Chapter 1

DEFINING YOUR COMPETITIVE EDGE

Think about the brands and businesses you turn to first. What about them has earned your loyalty? Your answer to this is probably very specific.

Your preferred big-box hardware store is probably not the one that "has good sales" or "has a wide selection," because you could say that about all of them. Instead, you might talk about the additional services they offer, the flexibility of their return policy, or their approach to customer service.

In the same way, your customers will not be won over by generic claims that your technicians provide fast, quality service. All your competitors say the exact same thing. Which means you can only win over customers if the buyer's game of "Eeny Meeny Miny Mo" lands on you.

If you want to stand out, you have to know what makes you special… what makes your company one-of-a-kind. In upcoming chapters, I'll talk about tapping into your customers' values and needs to identify opportunities to give them what no one else does. But before we get into that, you need to take an inventory of the aspects of your business that already set you apart. Let's take a look at how your business stands out in four notable areas:

1. Mission
2. Convenience
3. Expertise
4. Innovation

WHAT IS YOUR MISSION?

Many business owners in the home services industry don't spend much time thinking about a greater mission. Their personal goal is only to build a thriving company. They assume their target client only cares about receiving quality service. So why bother uniting their team around a shared mission as long as everybody does a good job?

Because customers actually care quite a bit about:

- Who they work with.
- The attitude you bring to the job.
- The potential "feel-good" benefits of working with you.

Just look at the super successful outdoor clothing company, Patagonia. They do make quality products, but they're not the only brand doing that. So why have they been leading their market for so long?

A lot of it has to do with their mission. Patagonia has always been ahead of the competition when it comes to reducing waste, using recycled materials, and manufacturing clothing that lasts. They talk about their environmental mission a *lot*. They even offer repair services so their buyers have the option to mend worn out gear instead of buying something new.

This goes over very well with their target customer: high earners who love the outdoors and care about the environment.

Believe it or not, the same strategy applies in the home services industry. If you visit the web page for any 911 Restoration franchise, you are pretty much guaranteed to see messaging that tells you we believe in turning every disaster into a Fresh Start. That is our core mission. We want to serve our community by transforming terrible experiences into new opportunities.

This stated mission has proven to be a powerful marketing strategy. Why? Because it tells customers:

- Our technicians bring a positive, hopeful outlook to a devastating situation.
- We see property owners as human beings in need of help, not as walking invoices.

- We don't just show up with wet vacs, do our thing, and leave. We apply our skills to create the best possible outcome for their property.
- We understand their needs and what it really means to fulfill those needs.

As an added benefit, our crystal-clear mission statement helps us get the entire team on the same page. Every franchise owner, every office worker, and every technician understands the importance of approaching their work with an attitude of growth and transformation. This makes them more compassionate to our clients and to one another. The buyer sees that. They feel better because they called us. So not only do we get the job, we also get long-term loyalty and advocacy.

So, what's your mission? How does your professional philosophy and purpose set you apart from your competitors?

If you've never created a mission statement and you really don't know what you're trying to do other than solve problems, ask yourself the following questions:

- *What deeper service do I provide, beyond cleanup or repairs?*
- *What customer interactions have felt especially meaningful to me? Why were those interactions so special?*
- *What is my purpose as an individual? How do I see myself making the world better using the skills I have?*
- *What legacy do I want to leave behind?*
- *How do I want my employees to approach their work?*

Some of these questions may seem extremely deep or exceptionally personal. But that's actually the point. In order to *truly* rally behind your mission, it has to be something that matters to you. The Fresh Start philosophy that drives 911 Restoration began with my own passion for new beginnings. Both my personal and professional struggles have taught me that our most devastating experiences can also be the most rewarding if we use those experiences to grow. I used that perspective to shape my company mission. Now it's part of our team culture and a central element in our marketing strategy.

Identify the mission that sets you apart. State it as often as you can... on every page of your website, on your business cards, on your trucks, everywhere. Even just adding one new phrase to your marketing can change everything for your business.

WHAT MAKES WORKING WITH YOU CONVENIENT?

Why is using your service easier than using somebody else's?

Convenience plays a major role in the decisions we make, even when it concerns property damages. In order to compete, you have to set yourself apart by being:

- More accessible than the competition,
- More available than the competition,
- Better at anticipating your customer's needs, and/or
- Better at removing the barriers that might prevent a client from pursuing your services.

If you are a home services professional, you may have trouble pinpointing areas where you excel in terms of convenience. As the owner of a water damage restoration company, I can tell you bragging about 24/7 availability is the same as a fast food restaurant boasting that they have a drive-thru. Yes, you definitely need to make sure people know about it, but it doesn't set you apart. It doesn't make you the obvious first choice. It only keeps you in the running.

At 911 Restoration, we make sure we also mention those convenient services that our competitors either don't have or don't mention in their advertising. Things like:

- Our guaranteed 45-minute arrival time
- Free visual inspection
- Free insurance consultation and filing assistance
- Mold remediation and property repairs so the client only has to make one call for a full recovery

With each bullet point, working with us looks easier and easier.

If you're struggling to identify the qualities that make your service uniquely convenient, take a step back from looking at the obvious details of how quickly you can arrive and how fast you can work. Ask yourself:

- *How do we (or can we) make it as easy as possible for customers to reach us?*
- *How do we make our billing, insurance, and payment process more convenient?*

- *How might our approach to service save the customer time or money in the long run?*
- *What system do we have in place to make sure the client knows where to go for answers and information?*

Remember, your customer's experience with your company goes well beyond the service itself. Take note of all the procedures and technologies you have in place to ensure a seamless process from the first phone call to the final payment. Then make sure your potential buyers know about it.

WHAT MAKES YOU AN EXPERT?

Why should property owners trust your quality of service over anyone else's? Where is the proof of your expertise?

Take a second to list all evidence of your expertise. That includes:

- How long you have worked in your trade.
- How long you have been running your business.
- The experience level of your staff.
- Any certifications or training required of your employees.
- Any affiliations with professional organizations.
- Awards you have received.
- Press and recognition.
- Customer reviews.
- Your company's size or rate of growth.

You get the idea. Now, you may not want to mention *all* these things in all your advertising. But I recommend making the list for a few reasons.

First, in order to sell yourself, *you* have to believe your service is top quality. As tradespeople, we are not prone to self-celebration. We get in there, get the job done, and move on to solve the next problem. But you need to be conscious of the remarkable skills you have so you can help *others* believe in those skills.

Second, having a list at your fingertips helps you tailor your message to your audience. When you're creating a Facebook ad targeting Baby Boomers, you might put more emphasis on your many years of experience. If you're advertising to Millennials on Instagram, you might focus more on the fact that you've been using eco-friendly carpet shampoo longer than anyone else in the local area.

On that note, it is a good idea to remember these more specific areas of expertise. For example:

- Are you an expert in environmentally conscious practices?
- Have you lived in the local area all your life and truly understand the needs of your neighbors and their properties?
- Have you served a lot of food service venues or historical buildings or any type of property that might require special treatment?

Details like these are also great to keep on hand for targeted advertising. It's a way to tell prospective buyers, "Your situation is special, and I'm the one who really understands that."

You don't have to convince clients you're the best in the business. You just have to convince them you're the best match for their needs.

HOW ARE YOU INNOVATING?

One of the best ways to stand out is by simply doing something new.

Do you have an automated SMS messaging system that tells clients when your technician is on the way? Have you created a system for drying water damage faster? What about an easier payment system?

As a business owner, you should always be looking for ways to offer a service that is:

- Better,
- Faster,
- For a better price.

Each time you find a new way to improve your products or services, make sure your customers know about it.

Now, that's not to say your customers need to know all the details. If you worked with a developer to create a new CRM tailored to the needs of your company... well, odds are good your buyer doesn't really care. It would be a huge waste to pay for an ad announcing you have the best CRM in the business.

However, you might want to mention to your customer that you keep notes about each visit so your techs come prepared, already knowing the history of the property and unique needs of the client.

> → Bottom line: you need to know what sets you apart. What qualities or services put you in a class of your own?

When you can communicate those distinctions to your buyer, you make it much easier for them to choose you over the competition.

IN SHORT

- Establish a clear mission that highlights the deeper service you provide.

- Show the buyer why your company is the more convenient choice.

- Decide how your unique history and skill set make you a true expert.

- Innovate often to stay ahead of the curve… and make sure your customer knows about it.

Chapter 2

UNDERSTAND THE WORLD OF YOUR CLIENT

t can be all too easy for home services professionals to underestimate the importance of understanding their client. Business owners in our industry tend to think they only really need to know two things about the customer:

1. They own a property.
2. They want to maintain the property at limited cost.

Another common assumption is that nuanced marketing is less important in the home services industry because most businesses in our field are absolutely essential to the customer. Plumbing, roofing, fire damage restoration... these services are not in the same category as hair salons or personal trainers. The buyer *will* invest in property repair services. No one gives themselves a few days to think about whether they want help with a backed up toilet. No one decides to live with black mold because they'd rather save their money for a boat.

As a result, it can be very easy to imagine the customer's mentality as one of urgent desperation. They need their property repaired, and they need it to cost as little as possible. And this is why you probably see a lot of the exact same marketing among your competitors… and yourself.

It's time to understand the client on a deeper level.

WHY YOU NEED TO KNOW YOUR BUYER BETTER

Just like in personal relationships, no good ever comes of *assuming* you know what's important to your customers. Their greatest priorities and biggest burdens may not be immediately obvious to you.

As an example, look back on all the jobs you've ever had. The ones you remember enjoying the most may not be the jobs that paid the best. They may not be the ones where you had the highest rank. More likely, the work you remember most fondly was the work that challenged you or was interesting or came with a friendly boss and supportive coworkers.

My point being, we even surprise *ourselves* when it comes to our deepest needs. So be careful what you assume about your customer's priorities.

If your local property owners are more concerned about quality work and the longevity of their home or business, you could lose them by overselling your bargain-basement prices. Or you might overemphasize industry recognition when your buyer would be much more swayed by the endorsement of their neighbors.

A deeper exploration of your customer's needs also helps you fine-tune your services and messaging to address those pain points that are often ignored. At 911 Restoration, we assumed money was a concern for nearly all our customers. But when we took a closer look at what our clients went through doing the restoration process, we realized they had an additional struggle when it came to payment: dealing with insurance. The back-and-forth with their provider, struggling to make sense of complicated policies, dealing with the details needed for loss itemization… filing an insurance claim is an exhausting under-taking. Add in the stress of a property disaster and many of our customers felt buried under a long list of to-dos. They were eager to get on with their lives but felt eternally stranded in the present moment.

So we added a free insurance consultation providing clear answers to all their insurance questions. We also made sure they knew we not only accepted their insurance, but we would also do everything we could to help with their paperwork and file the claim for them.

You see what a difference it makes to understand your buyer better? If we had never bothered to take note of what our clients went through when their property flooded or went up in flames, we would have been stuck boasting about good prices... which *is* a feature customers care about, but it really doesn't do much to set us apart.

Now that you understand the value of researching your buyers further, let's take a closer look at the type of information you should be looking for.

WHAT YOU NEED TO KNOW ABOUT YOUR BUYER

Let's walk through a few questions you should be able to answer about your target customer.

What demographics do you serve?

Demographics refers to details such as:

- Age
- Gender
- Marital status
- Race
- Ethnicity
- Education
- Employment
- Income

While examining these details about your customers can get tricky—you definitely want to avoid stereotyping and making assumptions based on things like gender, ethnicity, and education—you should be conscious of this information as you design your marketing strategy. For example:

- Age might influence which marketing strategies you use, such as print ads versus Instagram ads.
- Income might provide a clue about promoting affordability versus promoting high-end services.
- You will likely address different pain points depending on whether a property owner uses their property as a business, a vacation destination, or a home for their family.

You get the idea. Demographics can't tell you everything, but it's a good place to start.

It's also important to note that there will be some variation in demographics among local property owners. That's fine. Use that information to create highly specific customer segments and target buyers more personally online. For example, you can run a Facebook ad tailored for Baby Boomers while also running an Instagram ad for Millennial homeowners.

This brings me to the next question:

How does your customer communicate?
One of the fastest and easiest ways to make your customer feel seen and understood is by speaking their language.

Now, it's possible you live in a community where this applies in a literal sense. If you serve a region where there is a large population that speaks a language other than the predominant language, it might be worth it to translate some of your advertising, provided you have someone on staff who can communicate with them when they call.

But "speaking a client's language" can be as simple as mirroring their communication style. For example:

- Does the customer prefer quick, straight answers or a warm, personable exchange?
- Does the customer respond to humor or feel more comfortable with a serious, professional tone?
- If you're new to the area you serve, are you familiar with local slang and terminology?

Finally, for anyone who is an expert in *anything* (that would be you), this is perhaps the most important question of all:

How do you explain your services so the customer will understand the full value of the work you do?

When you spend your life thinking about air scrubbers and thermal fogging, it can be easy to forget that most people don't really know the difference. Get clear on what you need to say to your buyers to help them *immediately* understand how they benefit from your methods.

What is the customer's state of mind when they are in need of your services?

When a potential buyer reaches out to your company, what are they thinking? What are they feeling?

Your team does the same job day in, day out. Sure, the locations change, but over time, all clogged pipes and cabinet installations start to feel the same. You might forget the emotional component from your client's point of view.

Take a step back and really understand what else the customer might need to hear when they're searching for businesses in your industry. Ask yourself:

- *If they're calling for repair or restoration, what are they most worried about?*
- *If they need a contractor, what are they most excited about?*
- *What about this process seems stressful to them?*
- *What outcome are they hoping for?*

When you take a deeper look at a property owner's state of mind, you find your messaging changes. You might include more words of encouragement in your ad copy. Or you might put more emphasis on what hiring you means for the future of their property.

$\rightarrow$ Another valuable question: *What has your customer's experience been in dealing with similar professionals? Do they have any assumptions about what contractors or plumbers are like?* If so, how can you indicate through your marketing that you offer superior service?

When you know your customer better, you know what they need to hear when they're looking for services like yours.

What are your customer's deeper needs?
Remember this: you are never *just* repairing a roof. You don't *just* handle sodablasting or sewage removal.

The customer always has deeper needs. They might need hope, guidance, or a new beginning. And *you* need to be able to pinpoint those deeper needs so that you 1) can meet them and 2) create a marketing strategy that demonstrates that you understand those pain points.

How do you uncover those needs? Ask yourself things like:

- *What does this property mean to the customer?*
- *What losses have they already experienced?*
- *What additional losses are they afraid of?*

Sometimes it helps to read Yelp reviews—your own and your competitors. You learn a lot about what your client considers a good transaction. See if you can zero in on how those customers felt working with the company they reviewed, whether those feelings were good or bad. In the case of a bad review, what did the customer need but never get? For good reviews, note the need that was fulfilled.

Then consider what you can do to reassure buyers that you understand these deeper needs.

How does your customer make decisions?

Buyers almost always make decisions from an emotional standpoint. That includes you and me. We all like to believe we're rational and objective, but the reality is very different.

Consider truck commercials. We see that powerful machine splashing through rivers in the wilderness and *we want that life.* All that stuff at the end of the commercial about safety ratings and new features is just there to make us feel like our emotional choice is smart and logical.

So that's the first thing you should understand about buyers in general.

But I encourage you to dig deeper and understand the decision-making process of your client just a little better. Ask:

- *Does my buyer care about reviews and other forms of social proof?*
- *Do they do a lot of research before making a purchase?*
- *What values factor into my customer's buying decisions? For example, is it important to them to work with local businesses, small businesses, or entrepreneurs who are active in charities or the community?*
- *Is my client more likely to trust their gut or cold, hard numbers?*

Understand how your customer thinks as they approach a transaction and you'll know how to communicate effectively with them in their marketing.

CREATING A CLIENT PROFILE

Now you have a clearer picture of what you need to know about your buyer. The next question is: how do you gather this information? And what do you do with it once you have it?

Customer Research

There are several ways to learn more about your target customer.

The first is simple. Pay attention. Your existing clients can provide a lot of insight into the way they think. Notice:

- The questions they ask about your services.
- Which aspects of your service they complain about or praise.
- What they say in online reviews.
- Why they refer other buyers to you.
- Their mood before, during, and after receiving your services.
- The language they use when asking questions or expressing themselves.
- How they talk about their property and goals.

Also note the way other customers talk about their experience with the competition. Read online reviews for similar companies in your local area. What did clients love or hate about the service they received?

Keep an eye on local statistics as well. Even in small communities, it's easy to get locked into a bubble. If most of the homeowners you know personally or regularly serve are of a specific age, economic, or ethnic group, you might make the mistake of assuming that's the common profile of homeowners in your area. Research the demographics. Is there a part of town you're neglecting? Is your region evolving in ways you hadn't noticed? Should you design an additional marketing strategy to reach new customers?

Finally, I highly recommend delving into the world of online marketing if you haven't already. Not only can you create highly targeted ads designed for specific customer segments, you can also test and optimize ads in real time. It's a form of ongoing buyer research. If your ad about eco-friendly carpet cleaner underperforms against an ad focused on response times, you immediately learn something valuable about your customer's priorities.

Now, what do you do with all this information?

Your Client Profile

A client profile is a highly detailed picture of your target customer. *Super* detailed. If you're new to this concept, this will probably seem like overkill at first. But once you develop a customer profile for yourself, you'll see how much easier it is to design a marketing strategy when you have a three-dimensional view of the human beings you serve.

To create a client profile, you are going to turn all the information you gathered into one fictional customer that represents the perspective and behaviors of your target buyers. It looks something like this:

Name: Derek

Age: 42

Income: $160,000 (dual income household)

Job: Manages one of his father's three tech repair shops

Property Type: Single family home in Brentwood, Missouri (a family-friendly suburb of St. Louis), 4 br 2 ba, built in 2010, current market value of around $550,000.

Family: Derek has a wife named Jessica who works part-time as a web designer. Both grew up in St. Louis County and live within twenty miles of their parents. Derek and Jessica have three kids: Kayleigh (14), Addison (11), and Tucker (9). The kids are in a highly rated public school and are very active in extracurricular activities.

Hobbies: Derek values family togetherness and spends much of his free time trying to share his most loved hobbies with his kids. This includes going to the golf course, to the batting cages, and skiing. He loves getting together with friends, but at this point in their lives, "getting together" is more likely to mean family barbecues rather than boys' nights. When Derek and Jessica have an evening to themselves, they usually keep it simple—going to the movies or eating out at their favorite Italian restaurant.

Interests: Derek is a fan of contemporary country music, the St. Louis Cardinals, the St. Louis Blues, Marvel movies, and goofball comedies. He's still mad that the Rams went back to Los Angeles.

Values: Family, honesty, and hard work are all important to Derek. He knows he benefits from his father's success, but he hates when other people point it out. He is determined to build on the opportunity he has been given, proving his own abilities and commitment. Derek would not say he's the kind of guy who needs to show off his wealth, but in truth, he does care about demonstrating that he can provide nice things for his family, and he sees prosperity as evidence of personal responsibility and good decision-making. He also sees his own success as a legacy he can pass on to his children.

Property Goals: Derek and Jessica value stability and plan to live in their home at least until Tucker graduates high school. There is a high chance they'll keep the house long after the kids are grown so the kids can return to a place that feels like home for holidays and family get-togethers. Derek doesn't often think about selling the property and buying something better, but he does sometimes dream of selling the home to one of his children when he retires.

Property Challenges: Derek and Jessica bought their house as a new construction, which meant they had a few years with minimal repairs. They have only just begun to confront new problems in the last year, so dealing with repairs and maintenance presents a new challenge in terms of both cost and hassle.

Personal Goals: Derek hopes to partner with his brother and take over the repair shops when his dad retires. His father is focused on the local market, but Derek would like to see their business expand throughout Missouri and Illinois. He also wants to get all three kids through college without debt.

Communication Style: Derek values quick and clear communication. He likes to get answers right away, and if he can find answers online or get them through a quick text, so much the better. At the same time, he is inquisitive, likes to feel informed, and wants others to see him as intelligent. For this reason, he appreciates it when a service professional takes time to explain what they do and why. In short, roundabout sales pitches do not work for Derek. It's better to start with direct answers and use those answers to help him envision a better life.

Purchase Behaviors: He will try to bargain, but he ultimately cares more about having nice things than getting a good deal. He likes to make decisions quickly; if he chooses to "sleep on it," it likely means he doesn't care enough about the purchase and will let it go. However, Derek does have a bad habit of making major decisions without consulting Jessica, and he is becoming more careful about spending money if he's not certain she would approve.

That's… A Lot of Detail.

I know. But as you read it, you gain a pretty clear picture of how to reach this person, don't you? You begin to see how marketing to Derek would be *completely* different from marketing to Fiona, the retired theater arts professor in the Pasadena bungalow.

What you are tapping into here is a talent you already possess but never think about: the ability to change the way you communicate depending on who you are talking to. I would bet you constantly adjust your word choice, tone, and persuasion tactics depending on whether you're communicating with an old friend, a stranger at the bank, or your grandmother. If you want to excel in marketing, you have to do the same thing for your customer.

Now, you might worry that this level of specificity means alienating a large segment of the population you serve. Even if you serve a neighborhood that is full of Dereks, there are other property owners in your area who do not line up with this detailed customer profile.

That's why I recommend creating multiple customer profiles. Then, tailor your marketing accordingly. When you create a Facebook ad, design it with Derek in mind. As for your ad in the local independent newspaper, speak to Fiona.

The better you know your customer, the more you'll stand out.

IN SHORT

- Great marketing begins with a deeper knowledge of your customer.

- Research your buyer on a deeper level to understand their fears, desires, values, and mindset.

- Use this intel to create highly detailed customer profiles that inform your marketing strategy.

Chapter 3

DISCOVERING YOUR CLIENT'S NEEDS

In the last chapter, I touched on the importance of understanding the needs of your customer. Now we're going to zoom in on this topic and explore new techniques for discovering your client's most significant pain points and working them into your marketing strategy.

Every single purchase we make is about filling a need. It may not be a real need. It may only be something we *think* we require in order to live a safe or fulfilled life. But real or not, every single time we put down money in exchange for goods or services, we are hoping the thing we buy will make our lives better or easier.

A compression sleeve to alleviate knee pain. A car with more safety features to protect the family. A nicer haircut to become a more attractive person.

Because every purchase is about fulfilling a need, advertising is simply a matter of convincing the buyer that you are the best need-fulfiller in the market.

And this means you must understand what your buyer's biggest problems are. More specifically, **you have to figure out what the customer perceives their needs to be**.

Because they may not the needs *you* perceive.

Consider Derek, the hypothetical client we created a profile for in the previous chapter. Let's say you're a contractor. All your advertising is built around the promise that you know how to make home improvements that drastically increase the market value of the property. When Derek is ready to add an addition to his home, do you think he's going to come to you or to the contractor who promises to guide homeowners through creating a custom space that meets their family's needs?

He's going to go to the other guy, because—as we have established—Derek isn't trying to flip his home. He may *care* about the market value of his property, but his long-term goal is to create a home his kids will want to return to and possibly even buy one day.

The important point here is that Derek's priorities are not necessarily obvious. Why? Because there are plenty of homeowners out there who *do* care about continuously upgrading and selling so they can buy bigger, better properties.

→ Bottom line: you can't assume. You need to get to know your buyer's needs. And you need to look at two categories: practical needs and deeper needs.

DEEPER NEEDS

I'm going to start with deeper needs, because that's where your marketing messages should begin. Look at the construction of every memorable commercial.

Olive Garden promises togetherness and good times (deeper need) by offering a really good deal on food your whole family loves (practical need).

Kay Jewelers makes your love felt (deeper need) through quality diamonds (practical need).

Nike inspires you to be bold and resilient (deeper need) by… wearing great shoes? Buying a moisture-wicking workout tee? We don't really know for sure because most of Nike's advertising shows us the product but *doesn't actually talk about it.*

So, what is *your* customer's deeper need?

Another way to ask that question is:

> **What could you say in your first line of advertising that would make your client <u>immediately</u> imagine a better or easier life?**

As I mentioned earlier, 911 Restoration marketing puts heavy emphasis on our promise to give customers a Fresh Start after disaster. We know our clients see a lot of competitors promising to "fix" their situation quickly, using quality equipment and proven methods. But we also know that pretty much every property owner can be confident that their situation is "fixable." Water can be removed. Soot can be cleaned. Mold can be killed. But what customers don't know is whether they can dare to hope that their home or business will ever be as strong, beautiful, and pristine as it was before. Will this incident hurt their property value? Will their refuge always feel a little less perfect? All the hard work and financial resources they put into making their property a sanctuary… was it all for nothing?

Our marketing puts those fears to rest right away. We assure clients that we make their property new again. We can't undo the disaster, but we *can* turn the disaster into an opportunity to create a space that's even better than before.

So, what deeper need do your buyers have? How can you tap into that fear in the back of their minds? If you don't know, how do you find out?

Learning your clients' deeper needs takes some degree of insight. Odds are, they won't put those needs into clear terms. After all, when we all eat at Olive Garden or shop for Nikes, we don't think we're looking for anything more profound than free breadsticks or a good cross-training shoe.

But we are.

Here are some ideas for getting into your customer's psyche and hashing out the fears and desires they don't reveal directly.

- **Empathize.** Put yourself in your buyer's shoes. What would you fear most? What would you hope for? How would you want to feel after receiving service?

- **Examine the values of the demographic you serve.** Do local property owners care more about the sentimental value or monetary value of their home or business? Who else benefits from their property (family, customers, etc.)? How does the buyer feel about these people?

- **What do your prospective clients say in their reviews of businesses like yours?** What seems to make them feel most secure or appreciated? What makes them feel neglected?

- **What is the subtext of your own customers' feedback?** What might they *really* mean when they say that your technicians didn't listen or that they feel more appreciated by your team than the Other Guy's team?

I also recommend promoting a company culture that emphasizes open, regular communication. Design a system in which it's easy for your techs to report back about each job—not just about the service they performed, but about how the customer responded to the personal and technical aspects of the service. Did they seem happy? Did they provide any type of valuable feedback? Did they care about the extra services you added because you thought it would make their lives easier? Did they express any wishes that your company offered other services or add-ons?

If you've grown your business to the extent that you are no longer taking the truck out personally, you *must* be able to get these types of details from your crew. That means creating a company culture of trust and support. Your team needs to know it's safe and productive to discuss a bad client interaction as a growth opportunity.

Now, let's take a look at your customer's practical needs.

PRACTICAL NEEDS

In theory, identifying practical needs is easier than identifying deeper needs. But it's still a process that requires some critical thinking.

You may think of your customer's practical needs as the service you perform. They need a mold inspection. Or they need carpet removal. That kind of thing.

> But remember: your goal is to **stand out**. In order to do that, you have to think about the pain points no one else is addressing. Most likely, the problem that led your buyer to search for your services is a problem that affects more than their property.

As an example, think about a homeowner who calls 911 Restoration for help after a pipe burst. The big, obvious problem is that their property is flooded and now they're vulnerable to structural damage. They need drying out services and they need them quickly.

But if we widen our view a bit, we can see that this issue creates additional problems for the client, such as:

- They have to rearrange their schedule to deal with this problem.
- They may have lost valuable personal belongings.
- They may be scrambling to protect items standing in harm's way.
- They are about to lose *more* time trying to make sense of their insurance and filing a claim.
- Depending on the extent of the damage, they may have to find a place to stay for a few days while our technicians fully repair their property.
- Their insurance doesn't cover everything they need to make their home new again, and now they have to make some challenging financial decisions.

For our commercial property owners, the list grows even longer.

- They have to close their doors until the damage is repaired.
- The client has to find a way to make up that lost revenue.
- They have to ensure their property is up to code after this disaster.
- Etc.

When you look at the more expansive needs of your client, you are better equipped to prove that you really *do* understand their situation. You care. You anticipate their questions and you're ready with solutions.

Take a moment to look at the wide-angle view of your customer's predicament. List all the practical needs they have. Then, write down services you provide to ease their burden. If you can't think of any, create new ones. You'd be surprised what a big impact you can have with one small adjustment. You can't go back in time and rescue the antique clock your customer lost in the flood. But you *can* offer to walk them through loss itemization. Even that simple gesture tells the client, "We understand what you're going through, and we're going to make sure you don't have to go through it alone."

So you've identified the deeper needs and practical needs that your team covers. Now, how do you communicate these ideas to your customer?

ADDRESSING CLIENT NEEDS IN YOUR MARKETING

One of the first challenges you confront when you start putting these ideas into action is that you are now aware of *too many* needs. Your buyer needs immediate attention *and* skillful service *and* a great price *and* clear answers *and*…

The list goes on. So how are you supposed to create a concise ad that gets the point across in only a few words?

Well, in the case of a pay-per-click ad, print ad, or any other marketing effort that requires extreme brevity, you focus on one need at a time. This is where it helps to have a few customer profiles on hand so you can tailor your message for a specific customer segment. For your homeowners with families, you might focus on how your cleaning products are safe for kids and pets. For your business owners, you might talk about speed and attention to detail. For young professional homeowners, you might zero in on their desire to preserve or increase the market value of their property.

Make an educated guess as to which need ranks highest for your target client. Build an ad with that need in mind. Then, create another ad for the same customer segment that represents whatever need seems like a close second. Test both ads and monitor them closely. Which approach gets more clicks and conversions? Congratulations! You just learned something new about your buyer's priorities. Now try a *new* ad focusing on a *different* customer need. How well does *that* ad succeed against the current high performer?

If you could use a little more guidance on what it means to test and monitor ad performance, hang in there. We'll get into all that in a later chapter. Right now, I'm just giving you a big picture idea of how you can turn a long list of customer needs into simple, straightforward ads.

The next question is:

How do I write ad copy that demonstrates my team's ability to meet client needs?

This is where you forget everything you learned about constructing a persuasive argument in school. That whole thing about stating your position then backing it up with facts... it doesn't get you anywhere when it comes to marketing. Remember, people make purchasing decisions with their hearts, not their heads. And messages like, "You should call ABC Plumbing because we have 30 years of experience" do very little to stir hearts.

The general rule of thumb is to start by stating the benefit. Please note: a benefit is not the same thing as a feature.

A **feature** is a detail about your product or service. Free inspections, 24-hour availability, same-day consultations... those are features.

A **benefit** is the way in which your customer's life improves because of your feature.

Another way to put it is that features are about how awesome you are, while benefits describe how awesome the client's life can be. Guess which one hooks the customer?

The formula for emotionally engaging ad copy is simple:

> *"Enjoy [benefit] because of [feature]."*

Let's look at an example, one that addresses a deeper need directly.

Imagine you are a contractor and you want to create an ad geared towards young homeowners who are excited to expand their homes but are also worried that their lack of knowledge and experience makes them a target for dishonest professionals.

Your benefits-first ad copy might read like this:

> Build your dream home with confidence. We provide references, transparent pricing, and a free consultation.

Compare that with a features-first ad:

> We provide references, transparent pricing, and a free consultation so you can build your dream home with confidence.

See the difference? The content is exactly the same, but benefits-first gets an immediate response of, "Yes! That's what I want!" Features-first eventually gets a "Oh, yeah, I guess that is what I'm looking for"... assuming the customer reads that far.

Of course, you don't have to use that *exact* sentence structure. For a real-world example of creative benefits-first messaging, consider Apple's wildly successful "Get a Mac" campaign. You know the one—it's the commercial that always begins with a cool, casual Justin Long saying, "Hi, I'm a Mac." An uptight John Hodgman follows with "And I'm a PC." The commercial nods to a feature of Mac computers through creative messaging, like when a sneezy, virus-ridden PC warns Mac against getting too close and an unworried Mac replies that he doesn't *get* viruses. But it's the benefit that is always front and center, starting with the actors' physicality and tone of voice. You immediately see that PC is insecure and constantly vulnerable, while Mac is relaxed and always in control of the situation... which is exactly how people want to feel when dealing with complex technology that stores all their hard work, memories, and personal information.

Help the customer imagine what it would be like to have their greatest needs fulfilled. *Then* demonstrate that your company can make it happen.

IN SHORT

- Consider the deeper, emotional needs of your buyer.

- Identify practical needs beyond the obvious.

- Use those insights to design benefits-first advertising that shows you understand your buyer and provide solutions.

Chapter 4

BREAKING DOWN THE DECISION-MAKING PROCESS

So you know how your customers feel. Now let's talk about how they think.

What happens in the buyer's mind as they consider working with you versus a competitor? What steps do they take between realizing they have a problem and finally committing to a solution? And how can you strategize your marketing to make sure you're connecting with clients at the right time and in the right way?

These are complex questions, but fortunately, the decision-making process is fairly consistent regardless of your market and your target customer. I am going to walk you through the stages of consideration that lead your prospective clients to make a purchase, and I'm going to cover the most powerful methods of persuasion for guiding property owners through those stages.

First, let's take a look at the buying cycle.

THE BUYING CYCLE: THE WHEN AND WHY OF CUSTOMER DECISIONS

"Buying cycle" is a phrase used to describe the process customers go through as they decide which business to work with. As I walk you through the cycle, it's going to feel very familiar. Though the speed of the journey and the length of each phase may vary, you follow these very same steps whether you're choosing a toothpaste or buying a car. The phases of the buying cycle are:

1. Awareness
2. Consideration
3. Intent
4. Conversion
5. Loyalty

Let's take these one by one.

Awareness

The client becomes aware they have a problem that needs to be solved.

For many home services professionals, your customer comes to the awareness stage immediately through a disaster like a sewage backup or a roof damage. However, some businesses may need to design marketing that creates awareness. For example, a mold remediation contractor might share blog posts or advertisements clarifying the warning signs of mold or the risks of ignoring an infestation.

Consideration
The client researches possible solutions. This often means comparing prices, online reviews, bonus features or services, and more.

Intent
The client is definitely going to make a purchase. They look at all the information they gathered on your company and your competitor's services.

Conversion
The client makes a purchase.

Loyalty
If all goes well, the client is happy with the service or product they received. They return again in the future and may even become an advocate, recommending your business to friends and family.

What You Learn from the Buying Cycle
Do you see your own process in the buying cycle?

Think of the last time you needed a new pair of shoes. You realized your old sneakers were worn out (awareness). So you checked out the selection at your favorite shoe store (consideration).

You narrowed it down to the three best contenders and asked your spouse's opinion, knowing you'd be leaving the store with one of those three (intent). You picked a pair and made your purchase (conversion). And if those shoes served you well, you looked for others in that brand when it was time to buy again (loyalty).

But what does this mean for you as a business owner? How does understanding this process help you market your own services better?

Simply put, the buying cycle helps you give customers the right information at the right time.

Let's say you decide to put a coupon for solar panel installation in a mailer that goes out to new homeowners. What phase of the buying cycle is your target customer in?

Probably awareness at best, right? They either have not thought of getting solar panels or it's crossed their mind as a project they'd like to take on sometime in the next year or so. Most new homeowners want to ease into spending even more money on their biggest purchase, and details like furniture and security take priority.

So how do you talk to a buyer who is in the awareness phase... or even pre-awareness?

You help them see the problem and recognize you as a potential solution. This could mean highlighting:

- The long-term savings of installing solar *today*.
- A time-sensitive rebate or tax incentive they can't afford to miss.
- The emotional value of creating a true dream home… instead of settling for good enough.

Now, imagine you send a follow-up email to a prospective customer who downloaded your free ebook, *Solar Panel Installation: What to Expect*. That person is definitely in the consideration phase. They may have even moved forward to intent. Either way, you don't want to waste your words explaining why solar is a good investment. Your target buyer already knows the benefits. A better strategy is to share a customer testimonial, tell them about a unique aspect of your service, or offer an exclusive discount.

You can see how the buying cycle can inform your marketing in a powerful way. It also helps business owners like you and me understand that marketing is a process. We can very easily become wrapped up in a hopeless effort to say the exact right thing that drives someone to pick up the phone *right now*, right away. But as buyers ourselves, we know nobody does that. No matter how heartwarming a Campbell's Soup commercial may be, you're not going to leap up out of your seat and run to the supermarket.

But you might slow down in the soup aisle on your next grocery run. That's your long-term goal as a marketer... to be remembered and considered at all phases of the buying cycle.

Now that you understand the journey of customer decision-making, let's talk about some of the biggest factors that influence the choice they make between intent and conversion.

CONVENIENCE

Never underestimate the persuasive power of convenience.

Amazon knows this better than anybody. First it was free shipping. Then it was free two-day shipping. And now it's the always-too-easy "Buy Now in 1 Click" button.

Convenience plays into our day-to-day decisions much more frequently than we realize. Are you going to order the *great* Thai food from the takeout-only place with the ninety-minute wait time... or will you opt for *good-enough* Thai food from the place with free delivery in thirty minutes or less? Is it worth it to drive an extra fifteen minutes for groceries every week because the market in the next zip code has a slightly wider selection than the one down the block? Have you ever decided not to gamble on an online purchase just because the return process seemed too costly or complicated?

Now, there may be instances in the above scenarios when you would have chosen the more complicated option. Sometimes better quality or more options make the extra effort worth it. But most of the time, you just have to get through your day. You need to check that oil change off your list, you have to get dinner on the table, and you need to order the housewarming gift for the party this weekend. And because you're a busy professional—possibly a busy professional with a family—you need to get those things done as quickly and easily as possible.

It's the same thing with your buyers. They may not consider convenience a *top* priority, but if they can't see a big difference in service quality between you and a competitor, convenience may very well be the deciding factor.

Create that "click to call" button on your website or add the 24-hour chat feature. Promise a faster arrival than the other guy or a smoother billing process.

Make it as easy as possible to buy from you. Then make sure your prospective clients *know* how easy it is.

CONNECTION

Customers like to give their business to people they connect with. This could mean working with someone who:

- They know and like personally.
- Shares their values.
- Contributes time or resources to the community.
- Contributes time or resources to support causes that mean something to the buyer.

- Runs their business according to ethical standards the customer values.
- Has already proven to be reliable and honest.
- Etc.

It's extremely rare that a purchasing decision is strictly a matter of dollars and cents. People don't just want to make smart choices, they want to use their money in a way that makes them feel good.

We see this at work in obvious ways, like when there is a call to boycott a business who gives to a controversial charity or supports hot-button legislation. People who disagree with the business's position refuse to spend their money there, while those who agree double down on their support.

But even if you're not the type to get wrapped up in that sort of drama, you probably still buy based on connection… at least from time to time. You stick with the mechanic who takes the time to explain what's wrong with your car and tells you when you can save money by ordering a part yourself. You don't bother looking for a cheaper dry cleaner because the one you go to sponsors your kid's little league team. You might choose eggs or meat according to the package's claims about how the animal was raised.

> **Connection matters.** Whether your buyers feel a camaraderie with you because of how you treat them directly or they just get an idea of who you are through your marketing, that camaraderie might be the ultimate decision-maker.

This means you should approach your marketing with the all-important question: "How do I use this opportunity to create a connection with the customer?"

(Hint: You'll find advice on that in the next chapter.)

EMOTIONAL APPEAL VERSUS LOGICAL ARGUMENT

Emotion is a more powerful selling tool than facts and logic. I've said this already, but I want to take a moment to help you understand exactly what I mean by "powerful."

In 1962, Avis launched a campaign advertising their status as the *number two* car rental company. Logic suggests that this would be a *terrible* approach. Wouldn't a clear-headed consumer take that information as a signal that there was a better option out there? But Avis played the underdog card with the slogan, "When you're only No. 2, you try harder." With that one sentence, Avis changed the emotional storyline. They were the company that had drive. They had grit. They weren't on top, but they planned to be. When Avis launched this campaign, they were suffering from a $3.2 million loss. Only one year later, they had a gain of $1.2 million.

Nike's "Just do it" campaign has been going strong for decades now. But do you remember how it started? In 1988, when the brand was struggling to compete with Reebok, they aired a commercial featuring 80-year-old Walt Stack running across the Golden Gate Bridge. He tells the camera he runs seventeen miles every morning. "People ask me how I keep my teeth from chattering in the wintertime," he says. "I leave them in my locker." Then comes the title card with those three iconic words: *Just do it.* There is no discussion about the shoes. But there is humor. There is heart. And there is the deceptively simple call to action telling us to act, appealing to our braver selves, the selves that want to stop worrying or wishing or overthinking.

Nike soon eclipsed Reebok and made $8.2 billion in sales over the next decade.

Emotion-based marketing can be so powerful that it alters an entire culture. Almost every bride-to-be in the U.S. sports a diamond engagement ring, and that's because De Beers had to unload a stockpile of diamonds in an economy that was still recovering from the Great Depression and World War II. The iconic jeweler created the slogan "A diamond is forever," reinventing this stone as *the* symbol of enduring love. Before that ad campaign, diamonds were present in only about 10% of engagement rings.

Emotional engagement doesn't just influence a buyer's decision to buy or not buy. The Capgemini Digital Transformation Institute survey *The Key to Loyalty* (August–September 2017) found that loyal customers who are emotionally engaged with a brand spend twice as much on purchases from that brand compared to emotionally non-engaged customers.

Why is emotional marketing so effective?

It actually makes sense when you give emotions their fair due. Our emotions are more than feelings—they're a function of our unconscious decision-making process. And this function has evolved for our survival. Anger warns us of danger. Love and affection lead us to form families, tribes, and communities that make us stronger and safer than we would be on our own. Emotion is actually part of our rational decision-making process.

Now consider that the unconscious mind can process 500,000 times more information every second than the conscious mind can.

This is why emotional marketing is so essential, especially at a time when the human attention span is shorter than ever. You have a fraction of a second to make your prospective buyer care about your brand. Your emotional messaging will always reach them first. Not because they're irrational, but because their unconscious mind arrives at a decision long before their conscious mind has taken it all in.

This rule even applies when conscious decision-making is crucial for the buyer. While the homeowners we serve are eagerly looking for a sense of security and hope for the future, our commercial partners will always be a little more focused on fact-based considerations. For example, a real estate agent has a team and clients to answer to. When they recommend 911 Restoration for mold remediation, they can't just say it's because we turn every disaster into a Fresh Start. They need supporting facts. They need bullet points.

So we give them bullet points.

But we *start* with the promise of *control*. Control over their deal flow. Control over their income. In the unpredictable, if/then world of realty, we offer them *certainty*. Their commission checks will not be delayed by an endless mold remediation process.

You see what I mean? Every buyer comes to every purchase decision with an emotional need, even if they are not conscious of that need. By acknowledging and promising to fulfill that deeper longing, you do so much more than you ever could by going on and on about how great your service or product is. You capture their attention. You make the client *want* to see you as the most practical option.

This is where your logical argument comes in. While emotional marketing is your strongest tool, the buyer still wants details that help them see their preferred decision as the smart decision. So by all means, list your amazing features. But remember to do it benefits-first.

Another way to look at it is that you're telling a story, and the client is the hero. A lot of businesses make the mistake of framing themselves as the hero.

> *"We're great! We do everything perfectly and fix all your problems! We're the best!"*

A much smarter strategy is to focus on how they can be the hero for themselves and those around them by using your goods or services.

> *"Create the home your family deserves."*
> *"Get your life back on track by calling our 24-hour technicians."*
> *"Protect your greatest asset with affordable home security."*

Even a good call to action frames your buyer as the proactive power in this transaction.

> *"Save money and call today."*
> *"Click the link to take advantage of our free consultation."*
> *"Explore our website."*

We are all the heroes of our own stories, and a good marketer is sensitive to this fact. Your buyer strives to be a good property owner, a good parent, a good boss. Your business is simply the tool the customer uses to meet those goals. Frame your company as a clear means to reach emotional fulfillment and add enough practical information to make the buyer feel good about trusting you.

Toss in a little connection, convenience, and timing, and you're golden.

IN SHORT

- Consider where your target audience is in the buying cycle when creating ad messaging.

- Demonstrate how easy it is to work with your company.

- Create a sense of connection between your business and the buyer.

- Appeal to emotional needs first, then highlight practical features to support the customer's emotional decision.

Chapter 5

WHERE YOUR PASSION AND CLIENTS MEET

The topics covered in this chapter are essential for every business owner. But if you don't consider yourself the "marketing and sales" type, I am especially talking to you.

When entrepreneurs struggle with marketing, it is often because they see advertising and selling as a sort of performance. You're putting on a character, doing a song and dance, trying to draw the client in with wit and charm.

But that's not what marketing is. Not good marketing, anyway. If you want to connect with buyers, your best option is to just be *you*. Be authentic. Tap into your values, double down on your strengths, and lead with passion.

Property owners know when they're being sold to. What really gets their attention is when a business connects with them… when an entire brand seems to *genuinely* share their values and understand their struggle.

Here's how you can make that happen.

KNOW YOUR OWN PURPOSE

To succeed as a business owner, you have to start with *who you are*. What are your priorities? What brings you joy and fulfillment? Who do you want to be for yourself and your community?

The answers to these questions should inform everything you do, from your company mission and team culture to your customer service policies and marketing strategy.

Your passion and purpose give your work authenticity, and that is the most powerful selling tool you have. Not to mention, running a business is hard. There will always be seasons of struggle, and the only way you can get through it is if you are motivated by a mission more profound than building wealth.

So just for a moment, block out any thought of who your competitor is. Set aside all the customer needs you discovered in Chapter Three. These considerations do matter, but you ultimately need to determine how *they* fit into *your* purpose—not the other way around.

Block out some time to sit alone without distractions. Turn off all the noise of the outside world and focus on your inner voice. Entertain the belief that you are completely limitless. (In truth, as an adaptable human being with a great capacity for learning and growth, you are limitless, but it may take time to truly believe this. If you don't yet see yourself as limitless, pretend you do. And maybe consider checking out my book *How to Transform Your Mindset and Become a Self-Made Success Story.*)

Once you are in a focused, positive mindset, ask yourself:

- *In what ways do I find fulfillment in my work?*
- *How do I envision my business influencing the larger community for the better?*
- *What reputation do I hope to earn for myself and my team?*
- *Assuming I am limitless, where do I see my business 5, 10, 30 years from now? (Dream huge here… whether "huge" means franchises all over the world or an innovation that changes the industry forever.)*
- *What legacy do I wish to leave behind?*

Admittedly, these are some very big questions. You probably cannot answer them during an hour of deep reflection, especially if you haven't given these questions much thought before. That's okay. Finding and naming your purpose is often an ongoing process. If you're stuck, try noticing how you feel as you go about your work day to day. For example:

- **Did a specific employee interaction leave you feeling positive?** What was it about that interaction? What specifically brought you joy? Was it a strong collaboration? The opportunity to mentor a promising team member? An unexpected personal connection?

- **What about a positive customer interaction?** What made you feel fulfilled or proud about the interaction? Did you solve a specific problem or offer reassurance? How did that exchange reflect the way you see yourself as a member of the larger community?

- **When have you felt the deepest concern for a customer?** What type of client crisis elicits immediate empathy from you? Is it an elderly neighbor who feels her home and memories are lost forever after a fire? A business property owner in a financial bind? A young couple who genuinely want to be responsible homeowners but are completely clueless?

- **Read reviews of your competitor. What positive feedback would you love to hear about your own business?** Skip anything vague that indicates financial success, like "Would recommend" or "Definitely worth every penny." Look at the emotional outcomes, like "They made me feel secure."

- **Even note positive interactions with friends and family.** When do you feel genuinely helpful? When do you get the sense you have assisted someone in a way no one else could? What is happening in those moments when you feel you are in the right place with the right person at the right time?

Notice what drives you and inspires you, what interests you and fulfills you, what kills your spirit and leaves you feeling unmotivated or distracted. You will gradually begin to realize what's truly important to you. You will see a clear line between the work you perform because it's your duty and the effort you make because of a deep desire to contribute the best of yourself to those around you.

Try to turn those discoveries into a clear purpose for yourself and your business. Actually write out a statement about what your mission is as an entrepreneur and human being. Something like:

- *My purpose is to help my neighbors create a true home for themselves and their families.*
- *My purpose is to not only solve problems, but to educate and empower my customers to care for their property.*
- *My purpose is to spread a spirit of hope and possibility in challenging times.*

Then—when you know what drives you—return to that list of customer needs.

THE INTERSECTION OF PURPOSE AND NEED

Most likely, you will discover that by living out your purpose, you naturally address a significant customer need. In fact, your purpose-driven business will probably be able to serve several client needs.

And if you look back at the list you made in Chapter Three and can't find anything that intersects with your purpose, guess what? You are about to discover a need you hadn't even thought of.

That's the beauty of prioritizing your Why. Many of us have a funny habit of assuming a passion cannot be practical. The reasoning goes that if we love something, it must not be of value to anyone but ourselves. Nothing could be further from the truth. Human beings are communal creatures! Our deepest desires stem from a need to contribute… a need to offer something meaningful to those around us. Whatever you are passionate about, I guarantee you, it is of value to your buyer.

So if you don't see a need that intersects with your purpose, work the other way. Ask yourself what your passion reveals about the needs of your community.

Then, emphasize that intersection in your marketing. You can do this by:

- Stating the company mission or philosophy that communicates your larger purpose.

- Acknowledging the customer needs that land at that intersection.
- Choosing words or images that reflect your attitude toward the work you do.
- Mentioning features and benefits in a way that emphasizes your purpose. (For example, instead of "We promise a quick arrival and fast service!" you might say, "Discover instant peace of mind thanks to our guaranteed arrival time." Or even simply: "Your emergency is our emergency."

Not only do choices like these tell the client you understand their needs; they also reveal your values. Whether you're all about keeping homeowners safe with reliable roofing in a wet climate or your focus is on helping couples create more space for their growing families, your advertising shows clients you're not just in this for the money. You're not just here to build an empire or make a name for yourself.

You do what you do because you care about your community... the same community that stands at the center of your buyer's life.

This is what I mean when I talk about connection.

WHAT IF YOU STILL DON'T KNOW YOUR PURPOSE?

Work with what you've got.

You can probably at least name some vague motivator. Maybe you want to help people, keep people safe, or make dreams come true. In time, you need to find a more specific statement to drive your business and your brand message. But for now, these ideas give you a place to start.

The bottom line is to find a deeper goal and match that to your buyer's deeper need. Build self-awareness and clarity over time. Before long, you'll discover a more certain path and a more specific Why.

IN SHORT

- Take time to define your purpose and company mission.

- Identify the buyer needs and values that intersect with your purpose.

- Use that intersection to drive your marketing.

Chapter 6

WHERE TO FIND YOUR FUTURE CLIENTS

N ow that we've covered the who, what, why, and how of marketing, let's take a look at the where.

Where will you find your customers?

Or, to put it another way, where should you be advertising?

There are countless marketing avenues available to you. In bygone eras, the choice would have been simpler. Newspaper ads, local commercials, radio ads, bus ads... the list goes on, but not too far.

Here in the 21st century, the Internet opens up your options considerably. This includes direct advertising like pay-per-click ads and paid social media marketing. But you also have access to strategies that fall outside the realm of a simple sales pitch. Blogging, explainer videos, influencers… there is a lot to consider.

How do you narrow down the options? Which marketing channel carries the highest potential return on investment?

Let's take a close look at the most common strategies and how they may (or may not) serve your goals.

PROFESSIONAL NETWORK

Your first and most powerful marketing tool is personal connection. Remember, property owners want to work with people who are part of their community… people who share their values, support their neighborhood, people they *know*. At the very least, they prefer to hire people who are *recommended* by people they know.

So, how do you position yourself as a familiar and trustworthy member of the community?

Cold Calls

First, there is the dreaded—*but extremely important*—cold call. If you'd rather do just about anything except cold calling, I get it. Most home services professionals are uncomfortable making sales, especially when they're selling to someone who never asked to learn more about their company. But there are tricks you can use to make this kind of direct client outreach feel a little less daunting.

Preparation is key. Block out a designated time to make your calls. Turn off alarms and notifications, close the door, and make sure any employees or family members who *might* interrupt you know to stay away for an hour or two. One of my franchisees refers to this time as "The Golden Hour," and though he uses this grand title with a tone of humor, just naming it cements this designated time as something that carries importance. Who would dare disturb you during The Golden Hour?

When you schedule time to make your cold calls, establish a rule for yourself that this time is for actually *making the calls*. You're not researching clients or brainstorming topics for small talk. You are calling.

That means creating a list of names and numbers ahead of time. Be strategic. Consider which prospective clients are most likely to become a high-value account for your company. Also prioritize those slightly warmer leads—the target clients who may not know you or be looking for your services, but who might be more open to hearing your pitch because of a shared connection or common business partner.

Referrals

At the same time that you're reaching out to prospective clients, you also want to build relationships with other professionals. At 911 Restoration, we constantly pursue new partnerships with property managers, insurance agents, real estate agents, and plumbers. All of these people are frequently in a position to hire a restoration contractor or recommend one to their own clients. We want them to know about us and think of us as a company that will make them look good for sending their customers to us.

Having now built many mutually beneficial partnerships with other professionals, I can tell you this is an excellent strategy for achieving fast, sustainable business growth. That's why I encourage new franchisees to pound the pavement whenever they have a day without bookings. And I'll be honest with you: their responses to that suggestion tell me who is driven to excel and who is still clinging to their comfort zone. The growth-o-riented entrepreneurs spend the day shaking hands with every property management company in their service area. The others find some reason they *have* to be in the office that day.

For many home service business owners, networking is just as uncomfortable as cold calling. It's also just as necessary.

Do what you have to do to get psyched. Schedule the time in your calendar. Give yourself a pep talk. Watch an inspiring YouTube video right before you get started. Reward yourself with a short break afterwards. Remember what sets you apart… how you're going to fill the needs everybody else neglects. When you put it in that light, it's easier to think of your cold call or office visit as a gesture of kindness. You are going out of your way to offer a solution.

Everyone has a different motivation. You have to find the one that works for you.

Just don't hide behind your advertising. Take the time to market with your own voice.

ONLINE MARKETING

The first thing you need to do when choosing your marketing venue is refer back to your customer profile. Where are you most likely to reach this particular person?

Now, there was a time when you were unlikely to find certain customer segments online. Times have changed. While there are still some individuals who opt to flip through the Yellow Pages, nearly everyone consults the Internet when making a buying decision now. You *will* have to do some version of online marketing in order to grow your business.

In all honesty, this is great news. Online marketing has major benefits for small businesses. The two biggest perks are:

1. You can use analytics tools to see how your ads perform so you can continuously optimize your strategy. (More on this in Chapter Eight.)
2. The Internet offers several marketing opportunities that don't cost a dime.

Here's a look at the biggest online marketing channels.

Paid Marketing

Pay-Per-Click Ads

What it is: The concept behind a pay-per-click (PPC) ad is simple. You create an ad (most likely through Google Ads), assign keywords, and determine a bid—the amount of money you are willing to pay each time the ad is clicked. (A click takes the user to the web page of your choice.) Anytime someone searches one of the keywords connected to your ad, Google uses your bid and the bids of other businesses to determine which ads to show in the search results. If your ad is clicked, you are charged for that click, regardless of the outcome.

Who you reach: PPC ads are powerful because almost everyone conducts an Internet search when looking for a home services professional. Regardless of demographics, most people who are computer literate and have access to the Internet will go to a search engine for answers.

Paid Social Media Marketing

What it is: Paid social media marketing can take different forms depending on your chosen platform and approach. For example, Facebook offers comprehensive ad formats including image ads, video ads, carousel ads, and collection ads. You have the option to display your campaign anywhere from the news feed to your target audience's Messenger inbox. And you can even designate your desired result, whether you want users to click a link, engage with your content, or message you for more information. This platform also offers "boosts." A boost is exactly what it sounds like: you select an organic post on your Facebook business page and pay the platform to boost the visibility of that post. You set a daily budget, select an engagement goal, and Facebook gives you an estimate of how many people will see that post based on your set spending limit.

Who you reach: It depends on the platform. If you're going to advertise on social media, choose the platform where you have the best shot at connecting with your target buyer. For example, LinkedIn might be the best place to get exposure to local property managers, while Facebook is better than Instagram when advertising to retired homeowners.

Influencer Marketing

What it is: Think of influencer marketing as the new version of getting an NBA player to promote your soft drink. Through influencer marketing, you create a contract with an individual who has a large online following. They might be huge on Instagram, they might have popular blog, they might be a vlogger with a wide fan base... you get the idea. They raise awareness of your product or service in an authentic way, like posting photos, creating video reviews, etc.

Who you reach: You reach the influencer's audience, which means you'd want to do your research to make sure their followers are the type of people who would buy from you. In truth, influencer marketing is more common and effective for certain industries than for others. For example, a company that makes snowboarding gear could get a lot of valuable exposure by striking a deal with a snowboarder who has a strong following. A local plumber has significantly less to gain. Only a small fraction of an influencer's audience would be local, and it would come off as inauthentic if the influencer were to post about plumbing services when they didn't actually have a plumbing issue.

Organic Marketing

Organic marketing refers to any effort you make to generate leads without paying for your visibility. You still might have to invest in designers, writers, tech tools, and other resources. But you're not paying for ad space. The most common versions of organic marketing online include:

Search Engine Optimization (SEO)

What it is: SEO is a strategy in which you optimize elements of your website to ensure your site comes up first (or close to first) in relevant Internet searches. Basically, search engines scan your website to get a sense of how valuable your information is. Things that boost your search engine rankings can include frequent use (but not overuse!) of relevant search terms, images, and video. The SEO guidelines change constantly as search engines become better at distinguishing valuable information from meaningless fluff. Nowadays, the bots even note how easy it is to read and understand your website copy. Search engines use this information to decide how to rank search results.

Who you reach: Anyone who conducts an Internet search to find the services or answers they need. So… almost everyone.

Content Marketing

What it is: Content marketing includes any useful or entertaining content you share online that ultimately raises awareness of your company. This could include videos, blog posts, infographics, free ebooks, webinars, before-and-after photo galleries… you name it.

Who you reach: It depends on where and how you share your content. A strong content marketing strategy can help you reach prospective buyers early in the buying cycle. For example, a search engine optimized blog post on questions you should ask when interviewing contractors can boost your visibility to potential clients who are only in the early stages of planning a new project.

Email Marketing

What it is: Email marketing includes all forms of client contact that happens through email. Blasts, newsletters, special offers… it all falls under the umbrella of email marketing. Even with the countless advertising channels available in the digital world, email marketing continues to have the highest ROI.

Who you reach: The people on your email list. If you don't have an email list, start one. Include past clients, non-competing colleagues, and leads. There are also several ways to create a system for capturing new emails. This includes adding a sign-up form on your website inviting people to subscribe for news and special promotions. You can also offer a free product like an ebook or webinar that requires an email address in order to receive the item. However, you must give people the ability to opt out of emails.

Organic Social Media Marketing

What it is: Unlike paid social media marketing, organic social media marketing is just a more strategic version of what you do on social media as an individual. Build a following, connect with colleagues and clients, share information and content you think your audience will find helpful or enjoyable, and take the time to engage. That means liking and commenting on other posts, promoting and celebrating people you admire, and replying to comments on your own posts.

The 80/20 rule provides a great standard for sharing valuable content on social media. It's simple: only 20% of your social media posts should be geared towards selling. The remaining 80% should be helpful, informative, or entertaining for your target audience. Try to incorporate images or video as often as you can. Visuals tend to draw more interest and engagement.

Who you reach: Once again, it depends on the platform. But whichever platform you choose, organic social media marketing is a great way to humanize your brand. You can showcase company values, demonstrate your dedication to educating property owners, and express your sense of humor. Social media is one of the most powerful marketing tools of the digital age simply because it allows for a more direct and personal relationship with the clients we haven't met yet.

MARKETING IN "THE REAL WORLD"

Now let's take it offline. While online marketing is undeniably powerful, there is still a lot to be gained from getting the word out "IRL." (That's Internetspeak for "In Real Life.")

As you can probably guess from my introduction, I am a big proponent of finding creative ways to connect with buyers. I encourage you to think outside the box and look for unexpected opportunities to promote your brand and communicate your values.

You are likely already familiar with most of your offline marketing options. These include:

- Radio commercials
- TV commercials
- Print ads
- Mailers
- Coupons
- Fliers
- Billboards
- Bus ads
- Bench ads

- Trade shows
- Sponsorships for sports teams, community events, etc.
- Etc.

A rising trend in offline marketing has been **experiential marketing**. This refers to any event or opportunity that invites customers to actively interact with your business. There's typically less focus on the product or service and more focus on client connection. An example would be a plumber setting up a booth at a street fair with a marble run for kids to play with. You know... one of those toys where you connect the tubes and gears to create a journey for the marble. In the context of experiential marketing, the plumber might refer to the tubes as "pipes," but the ultimate goal is to embrace an opportunity to attract families to the booth and foster warmer relationships with the community.

The challenge of real-world marketing is that you have to think a little more critically about where you place your advertising dollars. You can create a Facebook ad knowing it will be shown *only* to homeowners between the ages of 30 and 65 who live within 30 miles of your business and love Jimmy Buffet. You don't get that same level of certainty with a bench ad.

Before you invest in any advertisement or promotional opportunity, ask yourself:

- *Will this ad reach enough of my target buyers to be worth the expense? (The business that sells advertising space should be able to provide demographics.)*

- *Will prospective clients encounter this ad when they are in the right mental state to notice and remember it?*
- *Do I need to adjust my ad in order to capture buyers' attention in this specific advertising context?*
- *Are any of my competitors advertising in this space? If so, how can I stand out? If not, is that a sign that this is an ineffective strategy for a business in my industry? Or is it an opportunity to reach a neglected market?*

→ **Bottom line: Be creative. Be bold. But think critically.**

IN SHORT

- You can effectively reach your target buyer through a combination of online and offline marketing.

- Cold calling is absolutely necessary, as is networking with potential referral partners.

- Online marketing offers unique opportunities to control who sees your ads and monitor performance in real time.

- Before investing in any marketing platform, take the time to make sure your chosen venue offers the best opportunity for connecting with your target audience.

Chapter 7

PUTTING IT ALL TOGETHER IN A STRATEGY

Do you feel a little like you're drowning in a sea of too much information?

Developing a marketing strategy is overwhelming because there are endless options. It's also easy to get distracted. You spend a month putting together a new content calendar, and then you notice that a competitor who focused on radio ads is suddenly drowning in business.

Don't worry. Like everything else in business, marketing is a process of learning, adapting, and growing. I am going to outline a framework for making the best choices you can make today. But the greatest success comes with the long-term process… with testing, observing, adapting, and refining.

Remember, it's about progress, not perfection.

Let's dive in.

STEP 1: WHO DO YOU WANT TO REACH?

By this point, you should have multiple customer profiles on hand. Start by zeroing in on the two or three profiles that are most likely to create rapid growth for your business. This could mean:

- A customer profile that represents a large demographic in your service area.
- A customer profile that represents buyers who are more likely to spend a lot of money on services like yours.
- A customer profile that represents prospective clients who are more likely to be open to services like yours at this moment in their lives or this time of year.

Once you've pinpointed the customer segments with the greatest potential to boost your revenue, move on to the next question.

STEP 2: WHERE WILL YOU FIND THEM?

Those super-specific customer profiles you created should give you some clear ideas about the best ways to connect with your customer.

Focus on three specific questions:

- *Where does my target client hang out, both online and offline?*
- *Where do they get their information?*
- *Where do they go to find services like mine?*

Remember, you want to connect with your customer at all phases of the buying cycle, not just when they have an immediate need for your services.

If you're working with a modest marketing budget, choose the marketing channels that appear to present the absolute best opportunity for raising your visibility with your target buyer. If any of those options fail to perform, you can always redirect your funds towards one of the channels you *didn't* try.

STEP 3: WHAT MESSAGE IS MOST EFFECTIVE FOR YOUR CUSTOMER IN THIS CONTEXT?

Once you've narrowed down your priority marketing channels, think about how you want to frame your advertising. Consider:

- What phase of the buying cycle is your customer in when they encounter your ad or content in this context?
- What is the greatest practical need this specific customer has at this specific phase of the buying cycle?
- What is their greatest deeper need?
- How does your purpose intersect with their need?
- What is the most effective way to communicate with this person? Think in terms of word choice, images, etc.

Use the answers to these questions to craft a message that speaks to your buyer's needs and emotions. Remember, focus on the benefits they reap rather than the incredible features you offer.

STEP 4: WHAT TOOLS AND TALENTS DO YOU REQUIRE TO EXECUTE YOUR STRATEGY?

Take inventory of all the tasks needed to execute your marketing strategy well. This could include:

- Market research
- Copywriting
- Web design
- SEO
- Photography
- Social media scheduling
- Video production
- Graphic design
- And much, much more

Also consider what services and tools you will need. These might include:

- Production equipment
- Analytics tools
- New software
- Project management tools
- Email marketing services

- Printing services
- And much, much more

Once you've established all your needs, ask:

STEP 5: WHO CAN HELP YOU?

Review the list of tasks you need completed. Is there anyone on your team who would be great at any of these jobs or is in a position to learn and expand their skill set? Do you have the budget to hire experts? Is there anything on this list you can do yourself—anything you have the time and talent for?

Assemble your team and invite their input on which resources are needed to execute your vision. Together, decide which tools, equipment, and services are essential and worth the expense. There are many design tools, project management systems, analytics tools, social media schedulers, and email marketing services that you can use for free when your business is still small. You will eventually need to invest in better plans or more comprehensive tools, but if you're on a limited budget, be strategic about which resources get the biggest upfront investment.

Also make sure your team is 100% clear on who you're trying to reach, the values and philosophies that define your business, and the message you'd like to communicate. Share the customer profile with every member of your team to ensure every aspect of the process is in total alignment.

Then get to work.

IN SHORT

- Define the customer segment you want to reach.

- Determine the best marketing channels for connecting with that person.

- Use both the customer profile and buying cycle to determine the best messaging for your marketing campaign.

- Decide what talent and tools you need to execute your strategy.

- Assemble a team.

Chapter 8

EXECUTING AND OPTIMIZING YOUR MARKETING STRATEGY

One huge mistake business owners make is executing their marketing strategy without a plan in place to measure its success.

I see it all the time… entrepreneurs in anguish because they put all this money and effort into designing new ads that fail to pay for themselves. My response to this is—first—"Are you getting more leads?" Because if there is a boost in leads but not in revenue, then the problem is *not* the marketing; the problem lies in closing the sale or collecting payment.

But if the business owner in question is seeing little-to-no boost in leads, then the next question is, "Do you have any idea why the marketing isn't doing what you hoped it would? What can you adjust to make it better?"

This is where a lot of entrepreneurs get exasperated. *"I don't know! I thought I knew what people liked, but I guess I don't!"*

Well... find out. Pay attention. Measure your results, look for clues, and try new approaches.

In other words, optimize.

Even when a marketing campaign is going great, optimize. Build on what's working. Create more campaigns that follow the lead of the one that worked well. Invest more of your budget in marketing channels that pay off.

Like everything else in business, marketing is a never-ending process of learning, growth, and improvement. If your current efforts are failing, don't get down on yourself; commit yourself to learning more and doing better. And if your current efforts are getting incredible results, push to boost your leads even more.

Here's how to make optimization an integral part of your marketing strategy.

TEST YOUR MESSAGING

Before you launch a new marketing campaign, you need to decide how you are going to test and measure the success of your efforts. How you do this will depend a lot on the marketing channel you use.

For example, you can track the results of any digital marketing campaign in real time using analytics tools. You learn details such as:

- Click through rate (CTR—the percentage of clicks an ad gets in relation to how many times it has been shown to buyers).
- How users navigate your site after clicking on an ad.
- Conversion rate.
- How many times your social media or website content has been shared.
- How often your brand is mentioned in social media and who's talking about you.
- Demographic information about users who click on your ads or navigate to your website.
- Etc.

This information is invaluable. If your ads or content are not getting the results you hoped for, you can refer to your metrics to find where the problem is.

For example, if your CTR is high but your conversion rate is low, the problem is not your ads; it's your website.

Or if the campaign you created to target young homeowners is getting a better response from retirees, it's time to re-evaluate both your messaging and your understanding of the market. Do you need to revise your ads to better connect with your

target audience? Or is it possible you made an error in identifying which customer segment is the likeliest to convert?

Another wonderful aspect of tracking analytics is that the vast
information you receive makes it really, really easy to conduct
A/B testing.

A/B testing is the process of releasing two different versions of
an ad or content and watching closely to see what performs
better. You can use this system to compare any number things,
including:

- Fear-based messaging vs. inspirational messaging.
- Financial benefit (low prices) vs. quality benefit (high-end materials).
- Cool color palette vs. warm color palette.
- "Click to claim your free ebook!" vs. "Click for exclusive tips!"

Through A/B testing, you have an opportunity to learn a lot
about what appeals to your customer very quickly. When you
test your ads and content on an ongoing basis, you are able
to continuously fine-tune your approach. Just remember, A/B
testing works best when you choose *one* factor to differentiate
between your A and your B. If you test a fear-based ad that uses
cool colors and emphasizes money savings against an inspirational ad with warm colors that focuses on quality, you'll have a
really tough time figuring out the exact reason one ad got more
clicks than the other.

So then how do you test your ads in the real world?

This is not quite as easy. There is (thankfully) no way for you to peer into your prospective client's kitchen to see whether they actually look at your mailer or just toss it into the recycling bin.

Nevertheless, there are a few methods you can use to learn more about the effectiveness of each campaign.

Call tracking is a great way to determine which campaigns are generating the most leads. This involves using a different phone number on each advertisement. As leads come in, your sales team only needs to note the number being used in order to determine which campaign or marketing channel led that customer to your company.

A similar trick can be done with online forms. Let's say you put out an ad inviting clients to your website to claim a freebie or book an appointment. Include a code they have to enter that is specific to that campaign. You can also create a unique landing page with its own web address—just make sure it's short and easy to enter.

There's also the classic "Show us this flier for a special discount."

And of course—and perhaps most importantly—there's the age old question: "How did you hear about us?" Make sure someone asks this question of every client who reaches out, whether that someone is a sales representative or a form the customer fills out to book an appointment. Keep track of the answer. This will help you learn very quickly where your leads are coming from. They probably won't tell you, "Oh, it was your PPC ad emphasizing your use of environmentally safe products, because that spoke to my values as a middle class Gen Xer here in Portland." But you will learn which marketing channels are bringing you the most traffic. You will also learn:

- How strong your reputation is in the community (Are you getting word-of-mouth leads?)
- How your website is performing (A response of "Internet search" probably means you're ranking well.)
- The level of brand awareness you've achieved (If someone needed a roofer and "just remembered your name," that's great.)
- Etc.

Pay attention, and over time, you'll gather more information about what works and what doesn't. These patterns help you continuously strengthen and adapt your approach.

They also help you get more out of your marketing budget.

MEASURE YOUR RETURN ON INVESTMENT

Testing isn't the only benefit of tracking ad performance. You also need to pay attention to the success of your marketing campaigns so you can measure your ROI.

Keep track of how much you invest in each campaign. This includes costs like:

- Hiring freelancers
- Time spent by any team members, including yourself
- Tools and subscriptions
- Equipment purchases or rentals
- Printing costs
- Advertising fees
- Etc.

Then, record the amount of money those leads ultimately generate. When it comes to marketing offline, you will probably not be able to get an exact number. But get as close as you can.

Regularly return to your numbers and compare them against one another. Ask yourself, "Am I generating enough money with this campaign to justify the expense?" If the answer is no, examine the patterns across all campaigns and see if you can determine a better use of your resources. Should you double down on a specific marketing channel, message, or approach? Do you think you'd get better results if you revised the existing ad, or do you have the sense that the venue you chose for that ad simply won't pay off no matter how you use it?

And then there's the most important question of all:

Is now the right time to make an adjustment, or do I risk canceling a great campaign before it's had a chance to yield results?

That's a tough one. Let's explore it.

WHEN TO COMMIT, WHEN TO PIVOT

First, you may need to give your real-life ads a little time before you can determine ROI with any accuracy. As a home services professional, you can't really sell your services to people who are not already planning to buy. Your clients either need you or they don't.

Now, ads designed for buyers in the intent phase of the buying cycle can give you a much quicker sense of performance. For example, if your CTR for a PPC ad with the keyword "plumber in MyTown" is still really low after a week or two, you might want to try a new approach. Most people searching for "plumber in MyTown" have a plumbing issue they need addressed *today*. They are actively looking to convert. And for some reason, your ad did not capture their attention.

But your radio ad? Your property renovation blog? That coupon you sent out to new homeowners? The new trucks with your new, value-focused slogan? These things exist largely to build awareness. The person who hears your commercial today may not call until eight months from now when a pipe bursts and your jingle about water cleanup resurfaces in their memory.

This is why it's so important to be strategic when planning your campaigns in the first place, and why it's so important to keep a close eye on your ROI. While you wait to get a better sense of how these long-term marketing strategies pay off, you can optimize your budget by observing and improving the performance of your short-term strategies like PPC ads.

While you're waiting to see financial returns on your long-term efforts, take note of how much you earn in terms of relationship returns. Note things like:

- Growth in customer engagement on your social media accounts.
- Growth in monthly visits to your blog.
- Growth in open and click rates for your newsletter.
- Etc.

In other words:

- Is your marketing helping you build relationships?
- Are you becoming known as a resource in your community?
- Do buyers see you as an expert and a trustworthy source of guidance?
- Do your prospective clients connect personally with your message?

You may not earn money for these victories today, but trust me: you'll get it in the long run. Trust and connection turn into sales, loyalty, and advocacy.

If your marketing strategy doesn't seem to move the needle in terms of earning buyer engagement, then yes: by all means, try something new.

But if you do feel you're building meaningful relationships with your audience, don't let modest financial returns make you panic. Focus for now on earning their trust, and the money will come.

IN SHORT

- Establish a strategy for testing your messages and measuring results.

- Track your return on investment—both financial returns and relationship returns.

- Pivot quickly when your strategy doesn't hook customers in the intent phase, but give customers in awareness and consideration time to build a relationship with your brand.

Chapter 9

BEYOND CONVERSION

t worked. You developed a thoughtful marketing strategy designed around your customer's actual needs. You executed the
strategy, tested a variety of approaches, monitored the results,
and continuously optimized your ads and content based on
customer behaviors. Now you're seeing a huge boost in leads
and conversions.

Don't get comfortable.

Remember, the best marketing strategy isn't about making that
cash register ding. It's about building relationships. And a happy
client is one of the most powerful marketing assets you have.

We talked about the phases your buyer passes through on the
way to making a purchasing decision.

Now we need to think about the two phases *after* conversion.

1. **Loyalty:** The client is happy and thinks of you first the next time they need services you offer.
2. **Advocacy:** The client spreads the word. They post a positive review, refer other customers, and eagerly sing your praises.

This is why relationships are everything. A meaningful relationship with one customer turns one appointment into countless appointments over a period of several years.

But to make this happen, you have to keep buyers coming back and you have to give them a reason to recommend you.

Let's talk about what you can do to make that happen.

KEEPING CLIENTS ENGAGED

First and foremost, provide outstanding service. That means you don't just offer skillful labor, you also find opportunities to connect with them personally. You follow through on your promises to meet their deeper needs, whether that's a matter of providing peace of mind or relieving the stress of their situation. If you book the job and your team provides adequate service, you leave the door open for a competitor to swoop in with better prices or a flashier slogan the next time that property owner is looking for help.

Second, look for ways to make your brand useful all the time— not just when your client is in a state of crisis. I don't necessarily mean adding services or products (though it's always worth considering). I just mean finding additional opportunities to stay connected and remain visible.

Think of it this way. You hire a mold remediation contractor. They come to your home, they do a decent job, and they leave you with their business card. You put the card away somewhere thinking, "Sure, they were good enough to hire again."

Then *years* go by before you need another mold inspection. You remember that the company you hired last time was fine, but do you remember their name? Do you remember where you put the card?

Not if they haven't given you any reason to think about them in the last several years. It's possible you'll recognize the name when you see it on an Internet search, but it's also possible you won't. Or that your search will lead you to a new contractor with a better deal or more positive reviews.

How do you avoid this fate for your company? How can you remain the go-to for your happy clients?

The brand awareness marketing you already have in place will carry some of the weight. If you maintain that connection-focused messaging, those ads will continually remind your current customers what your name is, how to find you, and why they love you.

This is also an area where social media and content marketing come in handy. Give your clients information and inspiration they can *actually* use when they're not working with you.

One of the biggest social media mistakes I see home service businesses make is that they fill their pages with things their buyers *do not care about*. They don't want to look at pictures of pipes. They don't understand inside jokes about industry trade shows. You will not get their follows or their engagement with content that only makes sense to you.

But that doesn't mean you have to post off-topic or start a cooking blog on your company website. Just find the intersection of their day-to-day interests and your area of expertise.

Can you offer them tips for keeping their home safer? For upgrading their investment property? For handling minor home repairs themselves?

Another possibility is to lean into your company culture. 911 Restoration's Fresh Start attitude is at the center of our social media content. We share videos, tips, and photos that center around the joy of creating a new beginning—whether it's an article about grade schoolers rallying to help a classmate in need or an instructional video about how to give an old chair a fresh look. It's all fun or useful, and none of it feels like reaching because we emphasize the uniting theme: a Fresh Start.

To keep customers coming back, make space in your marketing strategy for messaging that demonstrates your commitment to enriching lives... even when you're not being paid to do it.

TURNING BUYERS INTO ADVOCATES

The next step up from securing future business is inspiring your client to spread the word about you.

Again, providing outstanding service is the most important strategy here. Be so good that your clients are *excited* to give their friends your number.

Also look for ways to make it easy for customers to recommend you to others. This could include:

- Creating a referral rewards program.
- Sending a follow-up email with a link to your Yelp page or anywhere else you'd like them to share their review.
- Maintaining an email list where you can send links to your own content or special promotions that clients can pass along to friends who might need it.
- Posting engaging, shareable content on social media.

The marketing doesn't stop just because you closed the lead. Exponential growth comes by turning each client into a lead-generation machine. And how do you do that?

You definitely know the answer by now...

IT'S ALL. ABOUT. THE RELATIONSHIP.

If you want to be better at marketing, start with the way you relate to your clients. Don't worry right now about being clever or cool. Focus on developing the tools that will serve you best in all your advertising efforts:

Curiosity and empathy.

Be eager to learn more about your customers every day. Put your heart and soul into understanding their desires, fears, perspectives, and needs. Ask yourself what information they wish they knew and what kind of support they wish they had. Position yourself and your company as the solution they have been looking for.

I often tell my franchisees to be customer-obsessed. This is how we set ourselves apart, both in our advertising and on the job. It is always about the people we serve, never about us.

Start there, and I promise you'll discover the kind of growth you have been dreaming of.

IN SHORT

- Market to your existing clients as well as pro-spective buyers.

- Find ways to stay visible and relevant to property owners even when they don't need your services.

- Make it convenient and fun for your clients to spread the word about your business.

NEXT STEPS

Thank you for allowing me to share my marketing insights with you. This is one of my favorite topics to discuss with business owners. As you may have figured out, I am deeply passionate about marketing... because I'm deeply passionate about people. And connecting with people is what marketing is all about.

When you look at it that way, you can see that this one aspect of your business is part of a larger, interconnected system. If the goal of marketing is to build relationships, then every other department has to be on the same page, doing their own part to further this big-picture mission. Your sales team should reflect the values and benefits stated in your marketing. Your office staff and technicians must create a customer service experience that follows through on the promises in your ads. And *you*...

...you must be the communicative, growth-focused leader who promotes a unified vision and company culture.

No pressure.

It's a big job for sure, but I'm here for you. My team and I are constantly developing new resources to help business owners like you at Get Out of the Truck. We even offer many of our tools and guidance for free. Visit us at GetOutOfTheTruck.life for video instruction, ebooks, blogs, tools, and more.

I've also created a Facebook group so I can share my experiences and insights with you in a more direct way, as well as learn more about your journey. Find us at https://www.facebook.com/groups/getoutofthetrucklife. Join us, introduce yourself, and let me know how I can help you find greater clarity and direction as you build your empire.

If you enjoyed this book, you may also find meaningful advice in my other books:

- ***Get Out of the Truck: Build the Career You Always Dreamed About*** is a short, practical manual that covers everything you need to know to establish and maintain a fast-growing business.

- ***How to Transform Your Mindset and Become a Self-Made Success Story*** dives into the topic of the entrepreneur mindset. Learn how to get past mental roadblocks so you can think, live, and make decisions like a winner.

Both books can be found at GetOutOfTheTruck.life.

Finally, if there is any other guidance you need, please let my team and me know through the contact form on our website. You know my purpose and mission is to help others discover a Fresh Start, and that includes driven entrepreneurs like you. Your feedback helps us plan content that will serve our community better.

Good luck out there.

—Idan

www.ingramcontent.com/pod-product-compliance
Lightning Source LLC
Chambersburg PA
CBHW061148040426
42445CB00013B/1610